Cornerstones of Freedom

Building the Capital City

Marlene Targ Brill

CHILDREN'S PRESS®
A Division of Grolier Publishing
New York • London • Hong Kong • Sydney
Danbury, Connecticut

Library of Congress Cataloging-in-Publication Data

Brill, Marlene Targ.
   Building the capital city / by Marlene Targ Brill.
     p. cm.—(Cornerstones of freedom)
   ISBN 0-516-06633-1 (lib. bdg.)—ISBN 0-516-20066-6 (pbk.)
   1. Washington (D.C.)—History—Juvenile literature.
2. City planning—Washington (D.C.)—History—Juvenile literature.
3. Historic Buildings—Washington (D.C.)   4. Washington (D.C.)—
Buildings, structures, etc.—Juvenile literature.   I. Title.   II. Series:
Cornerstones of freedom.
F194.3.B75 1996
975.3—dc20
                                          95-40518
                                             CIP
                                              AC

French architect Pierre Charles L'Enfant was delighted by the sight of the Potomac River valley spread out before him. In 1791, rolling hills and thick forests lined the river's Eastern Branch to Tiber Creek. Tobacco fields dotted with farmhouses and slave cabins stretched inland.

But L'Enfant imagined a different view. Stately buildings fit for a king danced before his eyes. He pictured tree-lined roads, parks, canals, monuments, and fountains. President George Washington had ordered him simply to find a good place for Federal City. Instead, L'Enfant planned an entire capital, a home for the new United States government.

Pierre Charles L'Enfant

Only thirteen states existed when the country was born in 1776. Each state elected congressional representatives to govern the infant nation. Now, Congress urgently needed a place to meet. During the Revolutionary War (1775-83), British troops chased the U.S. Congress out of eight different towns.

Even after the war ended, Congress was not safe from attack. In 1783, Congress was threatened by its own federal soldiers armed with bayonets. They went to Congress demanding to be paid the money they had earned throughout the war. Defenseless, congressional representatives fled Philadelphia for Princeton, New Jersey. But they vowed to find a safe meeting place.

In May 1787, lawmakers met again in Philadelphia. This time, they wrote the United States Constitution—a list of rules to govern the nation. The Constitution explained how the country would elect its government leaders. It also directed Congress to establish a permanent capital on land that was separate from any state. But lawmakers disagreed about where this seat of national government would be.

Pierre Charles L'Enfant remodeled New York's City Hall into a new meeting place called Federal Hall. The first U.S. president, George Washington, took the oath of office on its

balcony in 1789. New Yorkers hoped the federal government would remain in their city. But southern states thought the capital should be closer to them. Bickering between the states dragged on for years. Finding a home for the government became a national joke. One poem teased:

The inauguration of President George Washington

> *Oh what a charming thing and pretty*
> *To have a noble Federal City.*
> *Then let us to the woods repair*
> *And build Federal City there.*

On July 16, 1790, lawmakers finally agreed on a central location. The federal city was to be somewhere along the Potomac River, between Virginia and Maryland.

President Washington chose the exact site, a 10-mile (16-km) square suggested by L'Enfant. The area contained part of Maryland, including George Town (later Georgetown), and land from Virginia, including Alexandria. George Town and Alexandria kept their local governments. Two smaller settlements, Carrollsburg and Hamburg, became part of the capital city.

Because the new city was inland and far from open seas, it appeared to be relatively safe from a surprise attack. But the city was not isolated. Ships could approach from the north, south, or west through the Eastern Branch, or Anacostia River, and Tiber Creek. The president already owned land in nearby Alexandria, Virginia, so he knew that this port city would be able to prosper through sea trade. As a lively business center, the capital would represent the strength of a new nation.

Maryland and Virginia agreed to give land and money to erect buildings. Additional money was to come from people buying land on which they would build homes and businesses. Washington assigned three commissioners to acquire land for public buildings. They decided to name the new city "Washington," in honor of the president. The city and its surrounding area formed the "Territory of Columbia." (The "D.C." in today's name "Washington, D.C." stands for "District of Columbia.") President Washington, a modest man, still called the project "Federal City."

An early map showing the street grid for the capital city along the Potomac River. Visible are the planned locations for the Capitol and the President's House (later called the White House).

*Benjamin
Banneker*

The president selected Maryland surveyor Andrew Ellicott to set city borders. Ellicott chose Benjamin Banneker, a self-educated African-American, as his assistant. Both men worked closely with L'Enfant and eventually completed his work. But L'Enfant's original design had the greatest effect on the city's future.

L'Enfant's original city plan matched the splendor of European capitals. But this city was different. The federal government held total power over early Washington, D.C. The president even appointed its city council, which had no votes in Congress. Washington became one of the few cities in the world that was created strictly for use by a national government.

L'Enfant wanted the nation's home to be "grand and truly beautiful." He planned a diamond-shaped wonderland of sweeping streets and stately buildings. He placed the "Congress House," or the Capitol, on Jenkins Hill, the city's highest point. As he gazed at the hill, L'Enfant reflected, "It stands as a pedestal waiting for a monument."

The President's House was to be a palace 1 mile (1.6 km) away from the Capitol. L'Enfant believed that because Congress and the president were separate branches of government, each should have its own space. L'Enfant planned for a grand mall with a 400-foot-wide (120-m) walkway to fill the span between the Capitol and the President's House. The two hubs of government would be linked by Pennsylvania Avenue. From Pennsylvania Avenue, several major boulevards would stretch throughout the city like spokes on a wheel.

At first, the President's House and the Capitol received the most attention by city planners. A contest offered five hundred dollars and a city lot for the best design of each. Irish architect James Hoban drew the winning design for the President's House. The three-story mansion was much smaller than the palace L'Enfant had planned. Still, the drawing did include the bold columns and interesting stonework that L'Enfant had envisioned.

William Thornton, an English doctor and beginner architect, submitted the winning design for the Capitol. His sketch showed a square center hall with rectangular wings on the north and south. Columns decorated the entry and a low dome topped the midsection.

William Thornton's winning Capitol design

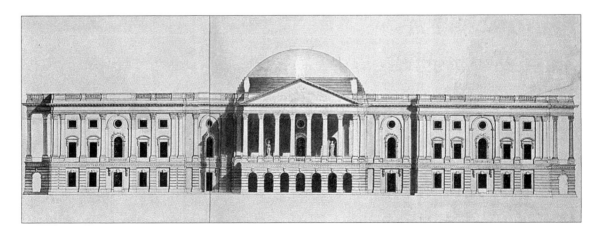

On September 18, 1793, President Washington led a group of masons to lay the Capitol cornerstone. The Virginia *Alexandria Gazette* reported that the stonecutters "marched two abreast in the greatest dignity, with music playing, drums beating, colours flying and spectators rejoicing." After the ceremony, a grand celebration was held featuring a barbecue of a five-hundred-pound ox and the city's first parade.

Building the Capitol building went slower than expected. Congress could not raise enough money for construction because it was having trouble selling city lots. Without enough income, the government was forced to borrow money for construction materials, tools, and wages.

A lack of laborers further slowed construction. The commissioners tried to find extra skilled workers in Europe. They brought in slaves from nearby plantation owners to perform unskilled labor. The wages earned by these slaves were given to their owners. Today, the nation is still troubled by the fact that the "land of the free" was largely built by the sweat of slave labor.

George Washington lays the cornerstone for the Capitol.

When lawmakers arrived in Washington in 1800, they found barely a shell of a city. The Capitol and President's House were behind schedule and still incomplete. They were surrounded by shabby huts used by construction workers. The only businesses in town were a brewery and a few taverns and boardinghouses. Cattle grazed on the uncleared Mall. Wilderness lay beyond. This was supposed to be home to about 14,000 people!

A view of Washington, D.C., in 1800

The second president's wife, Abigail Adams, became lost on her way to the city. Her coach driver passed through such wild country that he had trouble finding his way. Upon arrival, Mrs. Adams faced a rain-soaked swamp. Hogs sniffed through garbage piles. The city teemed with mosquitoes from the unfinished canal. Traveling was extremely difficult without lights, roads, or walkways.

Inside the President's House, conditions were not much better. Abigail wrote, "...there is not a single apartment finished...We have not the least fence, yard, or other convenience...[in the East Room] I make a drying-room of, to hang up the clothes in." Washington was a far cry from bustling Philadelphia or New York.

Despite the city's problems, President John Adams knew Washington was the heart of the nation. On November 22, 1800, he addressed Congress in the unfinished Capitol. He called the capital a great "residence of virtue and happiness."

But lawmakers found little hope for the city's greatness. Only the north Capitol wing was finished. So thirty-two senators, 106 representatives, and many other employees of the Library of Congress, Supreme Court, and circuit courts squeezed into a single, crowded space each day.

As this 1890s photo reveals, it took a long time for construction to completely replace wilderness in Washington, D.C. Here, cows graze in a swamp with the U.S. Capitol visible in the background.

The Capitol basement became so cramped that Supreme Court judges often heard cases in a nearby tavern.

Living conditions for the lawmakers were equally unpleasant. The closest decent housing was a long, rough ride away in Georgetown. Most government workers left their families at home, which could be hours or days away. Congressional sessions were brief so that members could return to comfort as soon as possible.

Thomas Jefferson (president from 1801-09) knew city life had to improve quickly. Foreign diplomats rated Washington a dangerous, hardship post. U.S. lawmakers threatened to find a new place for the capital.

Thomas Jefferson

Jefferson persuaded Congress to build a Center Market, a church, two schools, military barracks, and elegant homes. Money was allotted for streetlights, curbs, and poplar trees on Pennsylvania Avenue. Jefferson appointed Benjamin Henry Latrobe as architect of the Capitol. Latrobe completed the House wing of the Capitol with carvings, columns, and a visitors' gallery. The city was still small, and its main industry was still government. But citizens began to gain pride with each improvement.

The War of 1812 with Great Britain was a severe blow to the capital. L'Enfant's city design proved hard to defend. Fort Washington, on the Potomac's Maryland side, had been built to guard the capital. But British soldiers easily bypassed this blockade and invaded the seat of government.

The British set fire to every building in sight. The Capitol and the President's House were severely damaged; many other public buildings were destroyed. Only the Postal Office Building and Patent Office survived. A heavy rainstorm saved the city from total ruin.

After the war, Congress again debated moving government to a safer place. But the war had stirred feelings of respect for Washington as a national symbol. So rather than move the capital, lawmakers approved large sums of money to rebuild Washington.

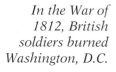

In the War of 1812, British soldiers burned Washington, D.C.

President James and Dolley Madison moved into the stylish Octagon House while the President's House was repaired after the war. By 1817, James Hoban had restored the President's House. The fire-blackened walls had previously been beige, but now Hoban painted the exterior white. Thereafter, the President's House was called the "White House."

Congress met in the Patent Office building while repairs progressed. In 1819, Boston architect Charles Bulfinch rebuilt the Capitol's Senate and House of Representatives chambers as Thornton and Latrobe had originally planned. Five years later, Bulfinch completed the center rotunda with its copper dome. Over the years, great artists added life to the building. They created wondrous paintings on the Capitol's walls

Visitors view some of the great artwork in the Capitol's rotunda.

and ceilings, and made magnificent statues of American heroes to stand in its halls. The Capitol is now a monument to the nation's art and history.

By 1840, only about 23,000 people lived in Washington. Builders had focused on a small area of the city's land in an area north of the Potomac. Congress assumed Washington would remain a small city, so it returned some unused land, including Alexandria, to Virginia. Since then, the city's size and shape have stayed mostly the same.

Each president added something to the flavor of government and the capital. Every four years, a president takes the oath of office. Beginning with Thomas Jefferson's second inauguration in 1805, a parade has been held. To this day, the president and his family walk or ride up Pennsylvania Avenue in a grand parade with bands, floats, and military units on display. In 1809, President James Madison added a new inaugural tradition. He sat in pew Number 54 at St. John's Church on Lafayette Square. Since that time, every president has followed the custom of attending a service there.

President George Bush and his wife, Barbara, walk up Pennsylvania Avenue during the presidential inaugural parade on January 20, 1989.

President Andrew Jackson ended L'Enfant's intended clear view between the Capitol and the White House. In 1833, the building that housed the Department of the Treasury burned down. Jackson ordered a new Treasury to be built east of the White House, jutting across Pennsylvania Avenue. Today, the Treasury Building is the third-oldest building in Washington (the White House and Capitol are older).

This view shows how the Treasury Building blocks the view from the White House (foreground) to the Capitol (background).

President Jackson also gave Washington the image of a "suitcase town." When he took office, he hired workers who had helped his presidential campaign, and he fired many who did not. He replaced more federal employees than any president before him. Jackson began the tradition of a president bringing in a vast new staff. Today, senators and representatives also bring large staffs of workers when they are elected. So every election, hundreds or thousands of people arrive in Washington as new employees, while many others leave the city because their jobs have ended. Because government workers constantly come or go, the term "suitcase town" applies to Washington, D.C.

James Smithson

In 1829, English scientist James Smithson died. In his will, he left his entire fortune to build a United States center of science and culture. Smithson donated his collections of books and minerals, along with a fortune—105 bags of gold. Congress accepted the generous gift, and in 1846 it established the Smithsonian Institution. In 1856, a red sandstone building was completed on the Mall to house the Smithsonian. Over the years, "The Castle on the Mall" expanded to include more than ten museums and galleries, as well as the National Zoological Park. Millions of treasures find their home at the Smithsonian.

An 1850s view of the original Smithsonian Institution, which today is surrounded by dozens of buildings on the National Mall

The Smithsonian's collection is so huge that most of it has to be kept in warehouses. This is why the institute is known as the "nation's attic."

By 1850, the United States expanded to thirty-one states with more than 23 million people. Washington's population rose over 40,000 people. Additional citizens and states brought an increase in senators and representatives. This meant that the Capitol became more and more cramped. Congress voted to enlarge the Capitol's two wings and replace the old rotunda dome.

Plans to improve the Mall and White House grounds were renewed, as well. New canals, roads, and railroads improved Washington's transportation. But the city had a long way to go before it became the business center of George Washington's dreams. Pigs, chickens, and geese still roamed the streets. The city's major canal gave off a sickly smell.

The National Air and Space Museum, part of the Smithsonian

Then, the Civil War (1861-65) turned the capital city into a military garrison. In the past, Washington had been a slave-trading center. In 1850, Congress banned slavery in the capital and ended slave auctions at the Center Market. Northern states wanted to outlaw slavery everywhere. But in the South, many states' economies relied on slave labor tilling the soil of plantations. The nation split apart when southern states left the United States and formed their own nation, the Confederate States of America. Four years of brutal war followed.

Washington became an armed camp. Forty-eight forts surrounded the city for defense.

A Civil War lookout post near Washington, D.C.

Troops slept at the Treasury, Patent Office, and the Capitol. Makeshift hospitals sprang up in schoolhouses, churches, and homes. Cattle, mule supply trains, and soldiers trampled streets and sidewalks. Sights and sounds of war were everywhere in the city.

The magnificent Capitol dome was completed in 1863.

With so many resources devoted to the war, many people thought the ongoing Capitol renovation should end. But President Abraham Lincoln insisted that Capitol repairs continue. "If people see the Capitol going on," he said, "it is a sign that we intend the Union shall go on." Workers did complete the new dome. And on December 2, 1863, a thirty-five-gun salute honored the new statue, called *Freedom,* as it was lifted to the top of the sparkling dome.

Washington's population expanded during the Civil War. Many people came to Washington for war-related jobs. Runaway slaves escaped from the South to the safety of the capital. People who approved of slavery fled south, leaving empty homes. Robert E. Lee refused to fight for the north and left with his wife, Mary Custis. Northern troops quickly occupied the Custis-Lee mansion overlooking Washington. After the war, the home became the center of Arlington National Cemetery. Thereafter, a sea of white grave markers filled much of the original estate. The cemetery stands today as a shrine to the nation's dead from every major war.

Abraham Lincoln's funeral procession through Washington, D.C.

On April 9, 1865, crowds of people built bonfires in the streets to celebrate the end of war. Five days later, John Wilkes Booth shot President Lincoln

in Ford's Theatre near the White House. Tearful mourners followed six gray horses pulling Lincoln's black hearse down Pennsylvania Avenue. Lincoln was the first president ever killed in office, and the country grieved.

An 1890s photograph looking up Pennsylvania Avenue to the Capitol

Rapid wartime growth left the capital with postwar problems. Criminals, war deserters, and the jobless prowled back alleys and stables. Word spread about the shameful state of the capital. The city badly needed repair.

In 1871, Congress voted to make the District of Columbia a territory, changing Washington's form of government. President Ulysses S. Grant appointed a governor and an eleven-person council, including civil rights leader Frederick Douglass and two other African-Americans. A Board of Public Works and a Board of Health focused on ways to beautify Washington, D.C.

Workers removed run-down empty buildings and disease-infested marshes. They installed roads and much-needed streetlights, sewers, sidewalks, and gas lines.

For the next thirty years, major planting projects changed the Capitol grounds to its current splendor. Every state donated a tree to the capital. They were a small part of the more than 60,000 trees planted citywide. The capital bustled with work crews, providing jobs for the unemployed. Government remained the city's chief employer.

Improved conditions attracted more people to Washington. By 1880, the population soared to 200,000. Housing prices skyrocketed with the demand. Major avenues housed foreign embassies, businesses, and members of Congress in magnificent mansions. Washington was becoming a world-class capital. Visitors praised the gleaming white buildings, lush parks, and shaded, paved streets. One of the most striking attractions was the Washington Monument, which honored the first president. The monument took decades to build and was finally

Laying the cornerstone for the Washington Monument

completed on December 6, 1884. Its marble tower rose 555.5 feet (168 m) high, overlooking the entire District of Columbia. The monument became a popular tourist attraction and symbol of the nation's towering strength.

Congress approved money for more buildings to help government conduct business. By 1900, government had built the Library of Congress to house national documents. The Postal Office Building and Departments of State, War, and Navy also reached completion.

But the Mall and surrounding areas were still a mess. Lawmakers recommended the city return to L'Enfant's original plan. Workers removed train tracks from the Mall to restore a clear view of the Capitol. They filled in swampland and seeded greenery to the Potomac River shores. The city of Tokyo, Japan, gave the United States 3,800 flowering cherry trees that were planted in the capital.

The Washington Monument today

The Lincoln Memorial

In 1922, the Lincoln Memorial, honoring President Abraham Lincoln, was finished. The commanding 19-foot (5.7-m) marble statue faced the Washington Monument. In 1943, Thomas Jefferson was honored with the completion of the Jefferson Memorial, set in a peaceful cherry-tree grove in southwest Washington. The presidents' memorials, the Capitol, the White House, and many statues and parks completed L'Enfant's original plan for the capital.

Meanwhile, the last century has seen many of the nation's urban problems strike Washington, D.C. During World War I and World War II, thousands of people streamed to Washington seeking wartime jobs. After the wars, many people stayed, straining the city's resources. Washington's population reached 487,000 people by the 1920s and peaked at more than 800,000 by 1950. Congress rushed to build new apartments, row houses, and office buildings after each wave of people.

Today, housing shortages, joblessness, and a lack of adequate schooling for lower-class families has created what some people call a "secret city" in Washington. Crime, filth, and poverty dominate the lives of many of the city's residents.

Despite its problems, Washington is still the vibrant site of government and a symbol of liberty. Washington has provided a special home to many moments in the civil rights movement of the 1950s and 1960s. In 1957, Rev. Martin Luther King led a march of 20,000 people demanding equal rights for African-Americans. Six years later, King returned to lead an even greater march on Washington in 1963. On the steps of the Lincoln Memorial, he delivered his famous "I Have A Dream" speech. More than 200,000 people were present on the Mall for this historic moment in the civil rights movement.

Martin Luther King at the historic 1963 civil rights march on Washington

The Pentagon (right), completed in 1943, houses the U.S. Department of Defense. One of the recent war memorials completed in Washington commemorates Korean War soldiers (below), dedicated in 1995.

Modern Washington, D.C., reflects the country's role as a world leader. Newer buildings, such as the Pentagon, are monuments to big government. And war memorials abound in the Washington area. In Arlington National Cemetery, the Vietnam Veterans Memorial and the Vietnam Women's Memorial are testaments to the men and women

who served and died in our most recent extended military conflict. In 1993, Washington saw the dedication of the United States Holocaust Memorial Museum, a testament to the millions of innocent people who perished at the hands of the Nazis during World War II.

Washington belongs to Americans. About 20 million people a year visit their capital. Some conduct business with government. Others view Congress in session or take tours of the White House, Capitol, and other historic sites. Tourism is Washington's second-largest business behind national government.

Visitors come to view L'Enfant's city plan—in granite, marble, plants, and flowers. U.S. history is embodied in the city's countless statues, monuments, parks, and buildings. The capital is the heartbeat of the nation, the place where history and government live.

An annual tradition celebrates democracy in the United States: a huge crowd thrills to fireworks over the Mall and the Washington Monument.

GLOSSARY

architect – a person who plans buildings

bayonet – a knife blade that is attached to the end of a rifle for hand-to-hand combat

Capitol

capital – home city of a country or state government

Capitol – the building where the United States Congress meets

diplomat – a person working for the government of a foreign country

embassy – the official office of a foreign government in another country

garrison – a military post; a central location where many soldiers are located

Holocaust – the killing of millions of people, primarily Jews, in Europe before and during World War II

inauguration – formal ceremony to place someone in office, such as the president

Patent Office – building in Washington, D.C., where government officials examine and keep records of every new invention

plantation – large estate or farm where crops are grown by people who live and work on the land

rotunda – a central area in a round building; the rotunda in the Capitol is under the building's dome

rotunda

suitcase town – a city such as Washington, D.C., where residents move in and out regularly because their jobs do not last a long time

territory – a region directed by its own legislature

TIMELINE

1775
⎫
⎬ Revolutionary War
⎭
1783

1787 U.S. Constitution signed

1791

1793 Capitol cornerstone laid

1800 U.S. government moves to Washington

President Washington chooses capital site recommended by Pierre Charles L'Enfant

1814

1817 President's House restored and renamed "White House"

British soldiers burn Washington during the War of 1812

1850 Washington's population is 40,000

1861
⎫
⎬ U.S. Civil War
⎭
1865

1871 Congress makes Washington, D.C., a territorial form of government

1884 Washington Monument completed

World War I
⎧
⎨
⎩
1914

1918

1922

1939
⎫
⎬ World War II
⎭
1945

Jefferson Memorial completed 1943

Washington's population is 800,000 1950

Washington residents allowed to vote in presidential elections 1961

Lincoln Memorial completed; Washington's population is 487,000

INDEX *(Boldface page numbers indicate illustrations.)*

PHOTO CREDITS

ADDITIONAL PICTURE IDENTIFICATION
Cover: The Capitol dome in renovation in the 1860s
Page 1: A 1941 photograph of the Jefferson Memorial under construction
Page 2: Modern Washington, D.C., from the air, showing the Capitol, the Mall, the Washington Monument, and the Lincoln Memorial (right to left)

STAFF
Project Editor: Mark Friedman
Design & Electronic Composition: TJS Design
Photo Editor: Jan Izzo
Cornerstones of Freedom Logo: David Cunningham

ABOUT THE AUTHOR
Marlene Targ Brill is the author of more than twenty-five books. She especially likes to write about places and faces that make history come alive. Her credits include *John Adams, Guatemala,* and *Extraordinary Young People* for Children's Press; *Allen Jay and the Underground Railroad* for Carolrhoda; and *Journey for Peace: The Story of Rigoberta Menchu* for Lodestar. Marlene lives in Chicago with her husband, Richard Brill, and their daughter, Alison.